You go to school every day.

So does Patrick.

Maybe you ride on a school bus.

So does Patrick.

After school you play with your friends.

So does Patrick.

In fact, there's only one difference between you and Patrick.

And it is a *big* difference.

Patrick is a dinosaur. A *big* dinosaur.

Patrick's friends are dinosaurs, too.

So is his teacher.

So are his Mom and Dad.

What's it like to be a student in a school for dinosaurs?

That's what Dino School is all about!

**Don't miss these other exciting series from**
**HARPER PAPERBACKS FOR KIDS:**

## VIC THE VAMPIRE
#1 *School Ghoul*—on sale now.

## THE KIDS ON THE BUS
#1 *School Bus Cat*—coming in November 1990.

**Dino School**

1

# A PUZZLE FOR APATOSAURUS

## Jacqueline A. Ball
### Illustrated by David Schulz

**Harper Paperbacks**

**Harper & Row, Publishers, New York**
**Grand Rapids, Philadelphia, St. Louis, San Francisco**
**London, Singapore, Sydney, Tokyo, Toronto**

*This book is dedicated to my wonderful parents, Joseph and Helen Ausanka, for a lifetime of love and support.*

Special thanks to Essex Elementary School, Essex, Connecticut, and particularly to the 1989—90 students of Virginia Sutherland and Cheryl McLaughlin—excellent brainstormers and outstanding jump ropers!

**Harper Paperbacks** a division of Harper & Row. Publishers, Inc.
10 East 53rd Street, New York, N.Y. 10022

Produced by Jacqueline A. Ball Associates, Inc.

Cover and interior design by Nancy Norton, Norton & Company

First printing: September, 1990

Printed in the United States of America

HARPER PAPERBACKS and colophon are trademarks of Harper & Row, Publishers, Inc.

10  9  8  7  6  5  4  3  2  1

# CHAPTER

# 1

It was nighttime.

Everything was dark.

Everything was quiet.

Suddenly there was a crash.

Then another crash.

A sound like someone moaning.

A sound like someone screaming.

A sound like something scratching at the window!

Trying to get in!

"Trying to get *me!*" yelled Patrick Apatosaurus. "It's a ghost!"

His eyes snapped open.

He sat up and looked around.

He was in his bed.

Sunshine was streaming in through the branches of a big apple tree.

*It must be morning*, he thought. *I must have had a dream. But it seemed so real!*

"Pete! Pete! Wake up!"

His older brother was sleeping in the upper bunk.

One giant foot dangled in the air.

"Uhh," Pete groaned.

Patrick pulled Pete's foot.

"UHHH! Cut it out!"

"But the sun is out. It must be late," Patrick said.

He threw back the covers. Baseball cards went sailing through the air. Patrick had been looking at them in bed. They were his prize collection.

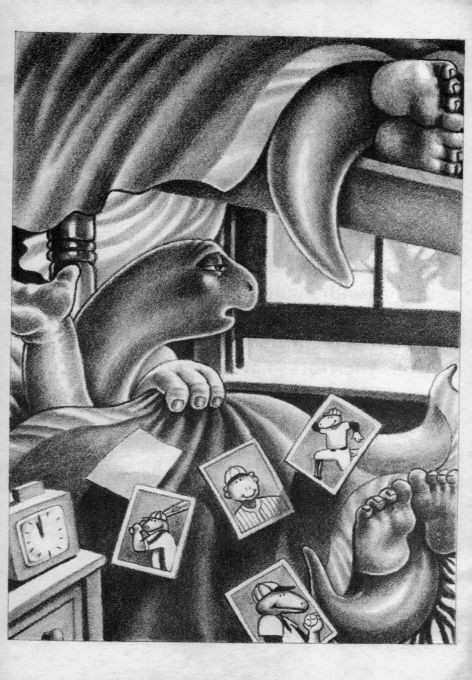

Pete sat up.

He looked at the clock.

He flopped back down.

The bed shook.

"It says midnight, stupid! We don't have to get up for hours!"

Just then Mrs. Apatosaurus hurried in. She carried two big brown supermarket bags. Each one was filled to the brim with sandwiches.

"Get up, boys!" she said. "There was a storm last night, and the power went off. The clocks have stopped."

Patrick was already out of bed. "Mom, I had the worst dream," he began.

"Tell me later, Patrick," his mother answered.

She put the bags down. "Here are your lunches. Peanut butter."

"But Mom, this ghost—"

"Quick, or you'll miss the bus," Mrs. Apatosaurus warned as she rushed away. "You don't want to miss the first day of school, do you?"

"No, Mom," said Patrick.

*What a way to start the school year!*

"No, Mom," Peter muttered in a making-fun voice.

Pete was always making fun of Patrick. Pete said that only nerds were as nice as Patrick.

But Patrick couldn't help it. He was naturally nice.

People didn't expect it at first. They thought someone so big would be a bully.

But Patrick was gentle and cheerful. That's why he had so many friends at Dino School.

There was his best friend, Spike.

There was Ty.

There was Hank.

All the girls liked Patrick, too.

Annette. Maggie. Sara.

Especially Sara.

In fact, everyone liked Patrick except Rex. But Rex didn't like anyone.

And no one liked Rex.

He was the meanest dino in school.

Probably the meanest in the whole town.

Maybe in the whole world!

But Patrick didn't want to think about Rex on the first day of school. He got dressed fast. He picked up his baseball cards. Then he dropped some. His hands were shaking a little.

*Maybe I'm scared about school*, he thought. *Like on the first day last year*.

Patrick put the cards in his backpack.

*Or maybe I'm still scared about the*

*ghost in my dream. It seemed so real!*

He packed a notebook his mom had bought him.

Then two pencils. A special pen shaped like a baseball bat.

He felt a little better.

He thought of Spike.

He felt *much* better.

Spike wasn't afraid of anything. Not even Rex.

Just then music blasted out of the radio. But nobody had turned it on!

Patrick leaped back.

"AAAAAH!" he yelled. "Mom! Dad! Pete!"

Pete came in from the bathroom. He was brushing his teeth.

"The power's back on," he said.

He turned off the radio. Then he saw Patrick crouched behind the dresser.

"What's your problem, fraidy-cat?"

Pete said. "You look like you saw a ghost."

Patrick sat on his bunk.

His stomach was doing flip-flops.

If only he could be brave. Like Spike!

# CHAPTER
# 2

Patrick and Pete caught their bus just in time.

But it didn't really matter. When they got to Dino School, everything was all mixed up because of the storm.

A giant branch lay across the "in" driveway.

Buses had to go in the "out" driveway.

There was no electricity.

The lights in the school hadn't come back on yet.

All of the clocks showed the wrong time.

All the confusion made Patrick feel even more jittery. Then he saw Spike across the ball field.

The friends hadn't been together for a month. Spike always went to camp in August.

"Hey, Spike!" Patrick called.

Spike waved. He ran toward Patrick.

Patrick put down his bag of sandwiches.

He pulled out his baseball cards. Spike would love the new ones!

Spike's real name was Stanley Stegosaurus. But everyone called him Spike because of the spikes on the end of his tail.

He was the coolest dino in the third grade. Even big dinos like Pete thought so.

Spike could bounce a soccer ball up and down his back just by shrugging his shoulders.

He could bat a ball with his tail. He could juggle apples with his tail, too.

He could stack sandwiches on his shiny spikes. He could punch notebook holes in paper with them.

Spike wore the coolest clothes, too. A worn jean jacket. A sweater with holes in all the right places. Patrick knew they were a special brand. Dino-Dude Duds.

"Hey, Pete," Spike called. "You seen Patrick?"

Patrick was surprised. "Huh? I *am* Patrick! It's me, Spike!"

Spike stopped right in front of him. He gave Patrick a friendly punch in the arm.

"Just kidding," he said. "But you

guys *do* look a lot alike, you know. You could be twins."

"No way!" said a girl's voice.

"Speaking of twins," said Spike, turning around.

It was Sara, one of the Triceratops twins. She was with her best friend, Annette Anatosaurus. Sara always wore bows on her horns. Today they were red.

"They do *not* look alike," she said. "Patrick's cuter. And *much* nicer."

Patrick felt his face get warm.

He kicked a rock across the grass. Hard.

"Point!" someone yelled.

The rock came skimming back. Sara's twin brother, Ty, was right behind it. He looked just like Sara. Except for the bows.

Ty gave the rock one last punt.

"Wasn't that an awesome storm last night?" he asked.

That reminded Patrick of his ghost dream. His stomach got ready to do more flip-flops.

"Not awesome," said Sara. "Mysterious!"

Patrick knew how much Sara loved mysteries. She was always looking for one to solve. Sometimes Ty helped her. But she was better at it. She told him that all the time.

"I heard wailing last night," Sara continued in a low voice. "Moaning, too. Sounds like a ghost would make!"

"Oh, it was only the wind," said Annette.

"I thought I heard a ghost, too," Patrick told Sara. His heart was pounding.

Sara nodded. "I wouldn't be a bit surprised," she said. She waved her hand at all the confusion around them. The buses pulling into school the wrong way. The teachers' cars parked in all different directions. "Look how mixed-up everything is. Ghosts *love* to mix things up."

Ty rolled up his sleeve. He looked at his watch. He rubbed it like a crystal ball.

"Ooooo. I see . . . I see a ghost . . . a ghooost in Room 211!"

Patrick's heart pounded faster.

Sara looked scared, too.

Ty raised his wrist. He looked closer at his watch.

"Wait. Sorry. It's not a ghost after all. It's just our new teacher."

"Very funny, Ty," said Sara.

The school had sent letters home in the summer. The dinos knew they would be in Room 211. But they didn't know their teacher's name.

Their teacher was new at Dino School.

Spike was grinning. "Well, at least tell us what our teacher looks like," he said.

Ty pulled his sleeve down again. "Sorry. Picture's faded."

"I don't care what our teacher's like," Sara said. "I'm just glad we're all in the same room again. Ghost or no ghost."

She smiled at Patrick.

He felt warm again.

He started fiddling with his back-pack straps.

"Let's just hope *he's* not in our class," Ty said. He pointed across the field.

A big, mean-looking dino was riding

into the schoolyard on a giant black bike.

He saw them looking his way.

He gave them a big, mean smile full of big, mean teeth.

He pulled back on the handlebars. The bike reared up on its back wheel.

*Like a horse*, Patrick thought. *A bad guy's horse*.

Then he started speeding right to-ward them!

"Oh, no! Someone let Rex out of his cage!" Annette cried.

"Watch out!" yelled Ty.

The dinos dived out of the way.

"Ha, ha!" Rex shouted. "Chickens!"

He skidded up to the bike rack.

He tossed a couple of little dinos' bikes over his shoulder.

Then he placed his own bike in the rack. Gently. Carefully.

"That big bully!" Sara cried.

"As I was saying, let's hope he's not in our class," said Ty again.

Even Patrick had to agree. His prize baseball cards were scattered all over the grass.

He bent over to pick them up. Sara helped him. She looked serious.

"Patrick," she said, "we'd better be careful today. Just in case."

BRIIIIIINGGGG!

Patrick jumped into the air.

"Easy, buddy," said Spike. "That's not a ghost. That's the bell."

The power was back on.

The first day at Dino School was beginning.

Beginning with a ghost.

Patrick shivered.

How would it end?

# CHAPTER
# 3

A sign on the door of Room 211 told the students to go to Room 311.

Standing next to Room 311 was a tall teacher.

She had a long neck. A *really* long neck.

Patrick counted three pearl necklaces on it.

She was holding a notebook and a pen. She was smiling.

"She looks nice," Patrick whispered.

"Don't jump to conclusions," Ty warned.

"Right," Spike agreed.

The teacher leaned down.

"Are you all in Room 211?" she asked them. Patrick thought she had pretty green eyes.

"Yes," Spike answered.

"Well, then—after you, gentlemen," she said.

She made a little bow and held the door open.

"This is really Mr. Pterodactyl's room," the teacher said. "We're just using it today. Some water leaked into 211 last night. In the storm."

"But where's Mr. Pterodactyl's class?" asked Patrick.

"In the auditorium. With the other second grade. Their teacher is sick and the substitute isn't here yet."

*More mix-ups*, Patrick thought.

The dinos shrugged at each other and went inside.

Other dinos were already there.

Sara and Annette were with Maggie Megalosaurus. Maggie was checking inside her lunch bag.

Maggie's lunch bag was *big*. It was as big as a laundry bag.

Everyone knew how much Maggie loved to eat.

"Oh, goodie!" she exclaimed. "Mom gave me enough Crunchum bars to share!"

"That must mean about a thousand," Ty whispered to Patrick.

Henry Ankylosaur was already in the room, too. His nickname was Hank.

"Hank! My man!" called Spike.

The boys ran over to Hank. They all started wrestling.

Hank got Ty by one of his horns. Patrick jumped on Hank's back. Spike grabbed Patrick's tail and pulled.

It sure was great to be back at school!

*Swish-thump. Swish-thump.* The teacher was tapping her tail.

"Boys," she said. "Let's settle down."

She snapped her neck to the front of the room. *She doesn't even need to move her feet*, Patrick thought. *Wow!*

"Find a desk, everyone. Sit wherever you like."

Sara and Annette dragged two desks over to the window. Then they pushed them together, front to front.

"Now we can see each other all the time," Sara said.

Annette clapped her hands.

"Let's us four move some desks way back," said Hank.

"Okay," agreed Ty.

He started to drag a desk to the back of the room. Patrick did the same thing.

Spike didn't move.

"Come on, Spike," said Patrick.

What was wrong with his friend?

"Huh? Oh, well, okay," said Spike.

The boys set up their desks to make a square. Patrick and Spike were on one side. Hank and Ty were on the other.

Patrick could see Sara lining up her pencils.

Suddenly her head jerked up. Slowly she looked around the room.

Then she smiled. The widest smile Patrick had ever seen.

"Guess who's *not* here?" she called out. "Rex!"

"Hurray!" said Ty. "Maybe they put him in the zoo where he belongs."

"Maybe they put him in jail," said Spike. *"That's* where he belongs."

"Nah. Who'd share a cell with that dude?" said Hank.

"No Rex! No Rex! No Rex!" Spike chanted.

Ty and Hank chanted, too.

Then Maggie. Then Sara and Annette.

In a minute the whole class was chanting.

*Swish-thump. Swish-thump.*

Their teacher's smile was now very small. And she wanted quiet.

"Class, let's say the Pledge and then we can—"

Just then Patrick felt the floor shake.

A piece of chalk bounced on the tray.

Maggie's lunch bag slid across her desk. She pulled it back.

"Mommy! I want my Mooooooom- mmmmmmmy!" a voice called from the hallway.

The floor shook some more. They could hear a loud pounding. It sounded like footsteps. Footsteps made by someone big—and in a hurry.

"Rex! Slow down!" a grown-up voice called.

"I knew it! I knew it was too good to be true!" said Ty. He buried his face in his hands.

Hank slammed the floor with his tail.

Rex stood in the doorway.

He was out of breath.

His T-shirt was all bunched up.

He looked mad. Patrick thought he looked meaner than ever.

"Is this your room?" the teacher asked. Her voice was calm.

"Yeah," he mumbled.

"Your name, please?"

"T. Rex." Rex stuck out his chin. "The one and only!"

"Good thing," muttered Hank. "What if there were *more* than one!"

Their teacher checked her list. "Yes, here you are," she told Rex.

Everyone groaned.

*Swish-thump.*

Rex snarled at them.

"Some other stupid list said I was supposed to be in stupid kindergarten!" he sputtered.

Sara turned around to look at Patrick.

"Mix-up," she mouthed. "Ghost."

"Well, it's easy to make mistakes the first day," the teacher was saying. "Especially a mixed-up day like today. Now let's stand for the Pledge of Allegiance."

After that they sang "The Star-Spangled Banner."

Patrick shut his eyes tight.

He was waiting for the high part. Where everyone messed up.

"O'er the lah-hand of the free. . . ."

This time it wasn't so bad.

"And the ho-o-me of the brave," the class finished.

Patrick could hear a grown-up voice above everyone else.

It was their teacher. She had a clear, high voice. Patrick liked it.

*Probably her long neck helps her sing*, he thought.

The teacher picked up a piece of white chalk. She wrote on the board: MRS. DIPLODOCUS.

"Can you all read my name?" she asked the class.

They tried. They sounded it out.

"Mrs. Dipl . . . lo . . . lo," said Maggie.

"Mrs. Diplod . . . lodo . . . ," began Patrick.

"Mrs. Dipl . . . ipl . . . ," read Sara.

"It's too hard," Maggie complained.

Spike was staring at the board. "Mrs. D. . . . Mrs. D.," he said.

"Wow, great idea!" cried Maggie.

Patrick was puzzled. What idea?

"What Spike just said!" Maggie explained. She waved her hand.

"Can't we just call you Mrs. D.?" she asked the teacher.

Mrs. Diplodocus looked at Spike. She seemed to be thinking hard.

Then she nodded. "I *do* have a hard name," she said.

Underneath her long name she wrote MRS. D.

Everyone clapped. "Spike always has the best ideas!" said Patrick.

Ty punched Spike in one shoulder. Hank punched the other one.

Spike smiled a little. Then he rolled a pencil down his back. He sharpened it on a spike.

The teacher wrote some more.

MRS. D.'S BE'S, she wrote.

"What does that mean?" asked Annette.

"You'll see," said Mrs. D.

She wrote BE KIND.

Then she wrote BE CURIOUS.

Last she wrote BE AWARE.

"We can add to the list any time," she said. "But let's add BE'S, not DON'T BE'S. It's much more fun to be positive!"

She picked up a stack of books.

"Now, will someone help me pass out the arithmetic books?" she asked.

Patrick and Sara got up to help. They

had passed out three or four when Patrick noticed something.

"These are spelling books," he told his teacher.

Mrs. D. shook her head. "I don't know how that happened. Well, pass them out anyway."

Sara gave Patrick a look. "More mix-ups," she said. "You know what that means."

After that, nothing went right.

Mrs. D. couldn't find the arithmetic books anywhere. And the social studies books were for Mr. Pterodactyl's class.

Diana Deinonychus had a stomach ache. She had to go to the nurse's room.

Finally Mrs. D. glanced at her watch.

"My goodness! It's eleven o'clock already. Time for gym class."

The dinos leaped out of their seats.

*Swish-thump*. *Swish-thump*. "Quietly, please. And *walk*. I'll be right behind you."

"So will someone else," Sara said to Patrick.

"Or some*thing*," he answered. "I think you were right, Sara. We'd better be on the lookout."

# CHAPTER
# 4

Mrs. D. left them at the gym.

"I'm off to see Ms. Brachiosaurus," she said. Ms. Brachiosaurus was the principal.

Ms. Iguanodon was the gym teacher. She wore sweatpants and a sweat-shirt.

A silver whistle hung on a chain around her neck.

Patrick could see Ms. Iguanodon had a problem. There were too many students and not enough jump ropes.

She told them that the schedules in the computer had been jumbled up when the power came back on.

Mr. Pterodactyl's class was in gym.

So was Mrs. Allosaurus's. *And* Mrs. D.'s.

"Okay, everyone," called the teacher. "I need you to really cooperate today. Share or take turns."

Hank and Ty shared a rope. They kept landing on each other's tails.

Rex had his own rope. He bunched it up like a whip. "I'm a lion-tamer!" he shouted. "Back! Back!"

Ms. Iguanodon held up her stopwatch. "See how many times you can jump in a minute."

Patrick and Spike counted for Annette.

"I can jump with my eyes closed," Annette cried.

"Thirty-five, thirty-six, thirty-seven, thirty-eight," Patrick counted.

Annette got all the way to forty-six. She only stopped two times.

"You're always the best at gym," Patrick told her.

"Better than those guys, anyway," said Annette. She pointed at Hank and Ty.

They could hardly get three jumps in a row. "Here," Hank said. He held out his end of the rope. "You try it alone."

Ty got to twenty-one.

"Doing fine, Ty," called out Ms. Iguanodon.

Suddenly there was a huge crash. The room shook.

Rex was lying on the gym floor. His jump rope was twisted around him.

He tried to kick away the rope. He

tried to bite it. But the more he struggled, the more tangled he got.

Everyone started laughing. They couldn't help it. But they muffled their laughs behind their hands.

No one wanted to make Rex mad.

Ms. Iguanodon blew her whistle. "This is hopeless," she said. "There are just too many of us. Let's go run some relay races."

Five minutes later the dinos were out in the school yard.

"Pat, be on my team, okay?" asked Ty.

"Sure," said Patrick. "Let's get Spike, too. And Annette."

"Where *is* Spike?" asked Annette, joining them.

They looked at the ball field.

No Spike.

They looked over by the swings.

No Spike.

"He was counting with me," Patrick said.

Just then Spike came jogging over. Patrick noticed that he was panting a little. His spikes were dragging.

"What are we waiting for?" Spike asked.

"For you," said Annette. "Where did you go?"

"To the office," Spike told them. "There was a message from my mom."

"Let's line up!" cried Ms. Iguanodon.

The teams lined up on the edge of the ball field. Each dino had to run across the field and back. Then the next runner would go.

The first runners leaned forward.

"On your mark . . . get set . . . GO!"

At first they were all even. Then Spike pulled ahead.

Pretty soon he was ahead by half the field!

"Go, Spike!" Patrick cheered.

"Wow! Look at him run!" yelled Sara.

She was standing next to Patrick.

Patrick got ready to run. He didn't want to lose Spike's lead.

Then Spike ran off the field—and right into him!

Patrick stumbled.

Everyone gasped.

Patrick didn't fall. But he staggered a few steps.

By that time their team was behind.

"Gee, sorry, buddy," said Spike.

"That's okay," Patrick called over his shoulder.

Patrick tried hard, but they had lost too much time. Even Annette couldn't save the day.

Two teams from Mr. Pterodactyl's class tied for first. Patrick's team came in second.

"I'm really sorry I bumped into you," Spike told Patrick. They were walking back inside.

"No problem," Patrick said. "It's hard to slow down sometimes."

"Especially when a ghost is pushing you," said Sara. "This day is getting spookier by the minute."

They were outside Room 311 when they heard something.

It was a scream!

# CHAPTER
# 5

Maggie was facing the board.

Her eyes were wide.

"What is it, Maggie?" asked Mrs. D. She was standing in the hall. But her neck and head were inside the classroom.

Maggie couldn't speak. She pointed at MRS. D.'S BE'S on the blackboard.

They still said BE KIND.

They still said BE CURIOUS.

But the last BE was changed.

It didn't say BE AWARE. It said:
BE WARE!

"Oh my gosh," exclaimed Patrick.

"It's got to be a joke," said Annette.

Nobody answered her. Everyone was silently staring at the board.

Mrs. D. twisted her necklaces around. She looked like she was thinking very hard.

"Wait a minute!" Sara suddenly shouted. "Look! Our desks are all moved!"

Sure enough, Patrick saw that some of the desks had been mixed up.

His own and Spike's were up front.

Ty's and Hank's were near the side bulletin board.

Sara's and Annette's were pulled apart.

And Rex's desk had been moved to a corner, where it faced the wall.

Hank started to laugh. "Someone just got tired of looking at Big Ugly," he said.

Luckily, Rex wasn't back from gym yet. Rex was always late.

"I knew it!" Sara said. She looked around the room. "I just knew it!"

"Oh, come off it!" exclaimed Ty. "Don't start on that ghost stuff again."

Sara turned and faced everyone. "But ghosts *do* sometimes move things around," she said. "Just like they mix things up."

Maggie looked worried. "I hope the ghost didn't take my Crunchums," she said.

She opened her lunch bag.

"Whew! Safe!"

"I'm sure Annette is right," Mrs. D. said. Her voice was very calm. "This is someone's idea of a joke."

"But why?" asked Ty.

"Yeah, why?" echoed Spike. "I think Sara's right. I think it *is* a ghost."

Patrick was amazed. "You, Spike? You've got to be kidding!"

Then everyone started chattering about ghosts.

"It's the old Bell Ringer. My grandma says he haunts the church on Route 154..."

"And *everyone* saw it! A real vampire—right in Centerbrook!..."

"My cousin in Chester knows a lady who's really a witch. And she looks normal!"

*Swish-thump. Swish-thump.*

"Class," said Mrs. D. "Enough. Please move the desks back. All of them. We have spelling to do."

"But the ghost might get mad," protested Maggie.

"Yeah. Why make waves?" Spike agreed.

Patrick was surprised again. Was Spike the Brave afraid of a ghost?

"Oh, come on," said Ty. "It's just someone fooling around."

He leaned close to Spike. "Besides, you guys don't want to sit up front all year. Do you?"

Spike put a giant eraser on his back. "What do you think, Patrick?" he asked.

Patrick really wouldn't have minded. But he didn't want to say so.

"Right," he told Ty.

Spike shrugged his shoulders. The eraser bounced all the way down to his tail. Like it was climbing down steps.

Mrs. D. erased BE WARE! She wrote again: BE AWARE.

On another part of the board she wrote:

## Spelling Word of the Day
### GHOST

She turned back to the class with a smile. "We may as well make the best of it."

# CHAPTER

# 6

By lunchtime the whole school was talking about what had happened in Mrs. D.'s room.

Even the teachers knew something was up.

Mr. Pterodactyl flapped by the boys' table. "Heard you had some excitement," he said. "Better watch out."

He grinned. He made his voice quiver. "Or should I say, BEWARE?"

He laughed all the way to the teachers' table. Mr. Pterodactyl loved his own corny jokes.

Suddenly Patrick felt scaly hands around his neck. The hands squeezed. They were strangling him!

"Ooooo! Ooooo! I'm gonna get yoooooooooou!"

Patrick reached back. He tried to pry the fingers away. But they were as strong as steel.

The ghost-voice came again. "Ooooo! Ooooo! I hate nice little creeps like yooooooooou!"

Patrick struggled with all his might. Ty and Hank jumped up to help.

"Lay off, Rex!" Billy heard Spike call.

He finally twisted away.

Rex gave him one last push.

Spike was hurrying to the table. Sandwiches and apples were stacked neatly on his tail.

"Why don't you look in the mirror and *really* scare someone?" he asked Rex.

Rex gave a mean laugh. Then he raked one enormous claw through Patrick's pile of sandwiches.

His claw made a big, ragged slash.

"Yuck," said Hank.

Rex licked his finger. "Peanut butter! Wimp food!"

Patrick took some deep breaths as Rex stomped off.

Maggie and Sara walked over to the table. "What a jerk," said Sara.

"What a waste," said Maggie. She was looking at the spoiled sandwiches. Her own tray was piled high with sandwiches and apples from her lunch bag.

"Ty," Sara said, "can I have my lunch money? I know Mom gave it to you this morning."

She looked down at the torn-up sandwiches. She wrinkled her nose.

"Not that I'm very hungry any more."

Ty reached inside his jeans pocket. He brought out his hand and showed her. Empty.

"Nope. The ghost must have stolen it."

"You do too have it! Give it to me, now!"

"All right! All right!"

Ty handed her a dollar.

"Brothers!" she said in disgust.

The girls sat down at the table. Annette brushed some crumbs from her seat first. She was very neat.

Then Annette opened a gigantic bag of potato chips. She offered some to her friends. Spike reached in to take a handful.

"Euw. Gross," Annette said. "What's that white stuff all over your sleeve?"

Spike looked down. There was a big patch of dusty white near the wrist of his sweater.

"Huh? This? I don't know what it is. I didn't notice it before."

He turned his wrist to see better.

He shrugged.

"Sometimes things come out of the wash like that. Mom says the soap doesn't get dissolved."

He brushed at the mark.

Patrick's appetite was back. He tried to eat his sandwiches around the scooped-out place.

"Do you think you can find the ghost?" he asked Sara.

"She probably doesn't even have one measly clue yet," said Ty. "Do you, Sara?"

"Yeah. Do you, Sara?" repeated Spike.

Sara smiled mysteriously. "Maybe," she answered. "Maybe even more than one."

Patrick hoped so. Between Rex and the ghost, this wasn't just a mixed-up day. It was a messed-up day!

One that he wanted to be over.

# CHAPTER
## 7

The ghost struck once more while the class was at lunch.

When the dinos came back, they found some desks had been moved again.

Spike's was back in the same place, up front. Others were scattered around.

Rex's was turned into a corner again.

Something was written on the board.

BE WARE! Just like last time.

But something new had been added.

Another BE.

BEFORE IT'S TOO LATE!!

Sara went up to the board. She looked closely at the writing.

The exclamation points were smeared.

"Someone sure was in a hurry," she said.

"Hey! Who's been messing around with my desk? I'll break his face!" Rex charged through the door.

"Ghosts don't have faces," said Annette.

Spike sat down. "Let's leave things alone this time," he said. "I mean, why bother to change all over again?"

Patrick was hurt. It sounded as if Spike didn't want to sit with him.

"I see we've had another visit," Mrs.

D. said. She was standing in the door-way. Her neck was stretched across the room to the board.

"The last one." She held up a key. "I just got this from the office."

"Locking the door won't help," said Maggie. She looked annoyed. "Ghosts can walk right through walls."

Mrs. D. bent her neck over to Maggie.

"But living creatures can't," she said firmly. "And I think our visitor is definitely alive."

Sara came up to Patrick. "I need to talk to you," she said. "Right away."

"About the ghost?" he asked.

"Yes. *If* there's a ghost."

Ty overheard them. "If?"

"Yes, if," Sara answered. She turned back to Patrick. "Come to our house after school. I need your help."

"Of course, you need my help, too," Ty was saying.

"Not as much as Patrick's," his sister replied. She smiled sweetly.

Patrick noticed Spike watching them.

"Okay," he told Sara. "I'll be there."

# CHAPTER
# 8

Later, Patrick was sitting with the twins on their front porch. They were having an after-school snack.

They were drinking chocolate milk. Gallon-sized cartons of it.

Four empty chocolate cream cookie boxes were on the ground.

Sara was sitting in the glider. She was pushing with her foot, rocking back and forth.

"This is my favorite place," she told Patrick. She took a bite of cookie. "Rocking helps me think."

Ty slurped loudly. "Okay, Miss Private Eye. What *do* you think?"

Sara settled back in the cushions. "Well," she said, "at first I thought there was a ghost because of all the mix-ups at school. But now I think that was all a coincidence."

"So there's no ghost?" Patrick wondered.

"Not a real one," Sara told him. "But I think someone was pretending to be a ghost."

"Who?" asked the boys together.

Sara rocked harder. The glider squealed.

"The one whose desk was moved to exactly the same place twice. The one with the chalk dust."

"Chalk dust?" asked Ty.

"On his sleeve. At lunch," said Sara.

Patrick suddenly knew who Sara was talking about. But it couldn't be!

Ty looked as surprised as Patrick felt. But he nodded his head slowly.

"It all fits together," he said. "He was late between jumping rope and the relay race. And he came in after the rest of us to lunch. So he had time to do everything."

"It's Spike," said Sara quietly. "Don't you think so, Patrick?"

"I—I don't know," Patrick said. Why would Spike pretend to be *anything*? He was so great the way he was!

"Well, don't *you* think he was acting funny today?"

Patrick finished his carton of milk. He opened another. Then he sighed. Sara sure was a good detective.

"Okay, he *was* kind of weird all day. First he thought I was my brother Pete. Then you saw how he smacked into me at the race. And he didn't want to move his desk back, either. He acted scared of the ghost."

Patrick made a face. "But Spike isn't scared of anything! I thought he just didn't want to sit with me!"

He could feel a big lump in his throat. He hoped it wouldn't turn into tears.

Sara frowned. She rocked harder.

"That couldn't be it. But why *would* he want to sit up front?"

"Why would anyone?" asked Ty.

Patrick scratched his head. "My grandma always sits up close to the TV. Especially when she forgets her—"

Sara jumped up. The glider banged against the side of the house.

63

"Her glasses!" she cried. "Maybe Spike *wasn't* scared. Maybe he just needs glasses. That could be why he ran into you, Patrick. And why he thought you were Pete. And why he couldn't read practically any of Mrs. D.'s long name."

Ty broke in. "Yeah. That could be why he kept moving the desks. He wanted to be in the front so he could see the board. It had nothing to do with you, Pat."

Patrick was shocked. "Then why doesn't he just get some glasses?"

"Right! Why make up some crazy ghost story?" said Ty.

Sara was heading into the house. "Beats me," she said. "But I'm going to phone the only person who can tell us. Sometimes even the best detectives need a little help."

Half an hour later, Spike was on the porch with his friends.

"What's up, Sara?" he asked. "You said it was important."

"She figured out who the ghost is," said Patrick.

Spike raised his eyebrows. He plopped down in a wicker chair. He was careful to drape his tail over the back of it first.

"Oh, yeah? Who?"

"You," answered Sara.

"Yes, Y-O-U," Ty said. "She also figured out that you did it because you need glasses."

Spike was very quiet.

"But why didn't you just buy some glasses?" asked Patrick. "We don't get it."

Spike started tracing circles on the floor with one big toenail.

"Okay," he finally said. "You're right. At camp I kept striking out because the ball looked blurry. The doctor at camp said I needed glasses. She sent Mom a prescription. Mom's taking me to the mall to get glasses tonight. At See-o-Saurus."

"So?" said Sara. "What's the problem?"

"I still don't get it," said Patrick.

"Neither do I," said Ty. "Lots of people wear glasses."

Spike got up. He picked up three empty milk cartons with his tail. He started juggling them.

They fell down. Clunkity-clunk.

"Not lots of people like me!" he said. "Lots of people like my brother Sam. All he does is sit around and read. I don't want to be like him. So I decided I'd never wear them at school, even if

Mom bought them. When you guys talked about ghosts this morning, I made my plan."

"But you'd never be like Sam or anyone else!" Patrick cried.

Spike speared one of the cartons. Then another. Then the third.

"I was afraid you guys might think I was weird or something, you know? That maybe you wouldn't like me any more if I looked different."

Patrick was surprised. How could Spike think his friends would let him down like that?

"Come on, man," Ty said.

"Of course that's not true!" exclaimed Sara.

"No way!" said Patrick.

Spike didn't look convinced. He was punching rows of little holes in the cartons.

Sara clapped her hands. "I know! We'll all go with you to the mall."

"Right!" said Ty. "We'll help you find some really *cool* glasses."

"Yeah," said Patrick. "Cool enough even for you!"

Spike flipped the cartons into a corner. "Okay, okay. I'll ask Mom if you can all come." He headed inside toward the phone. "But I still don't want them."

"It'll be okay," Patrick said to him. "You'll see."

"In more ways than one," agreed Ty. "Ha, ha. Joke."

Sara groaned.

# CHAPTER
## 9

There was no storm that night.

The second day of Dino School was sunny and bright.

The fallen branch had been taken away.

The buses went in the "in" driveway. They went out the "out" driveway.

Teachers and students strolled into the building.

All the clocks were set to the right time.

Everything was back to normal.

The sign outside Room 311 said Room 211 was ready for students.

Mrs. D. was behind her desk when her students came in.

"Good morning, Sara. Good morning, Patrick, Tyrone."

Today black velvet ribbons were wound around her neck. Five of them, Patrick counted.

Spike wasn't there yet. "He'd better not chicken out," said Ty.

"I hope he can find the new room," said Patrick.

Suddenly there was a lot of noise in the hall.

"Wow! All *right!*"

"Awesome! The kind you can wear inside!"

"Yes! Yes!"

Spike came into the room.

He wore a striped T-shirt.

A leather jacket.

And the coolest pair of sunglasses anyone had ever seen.

Mrs. D. gave him a bright smile. "Good morning, Stanley," she said. "You're looking wide awake."

"Wow, what great shades!" Hank cried. "Where'd you get them?"

"I want some too!" said Maggie.

"Me, too!" said Annette.

Everyone gathered around Spike to look at his glasses.

"They get lighter when I'm inside," he explained. "And darker when I'm out."

"You lucky!" said Hank. "I wish *I* needed glasses."

*Swish-thump. Swish-thump.*

"Let's take our places," said Mrs. D. "Stanley, your desk is waiting for you."

She pointed to the rear of the room.

Four desks were in a square. As far back as they could be.

Spike gave a thumbs-up sign. He ran to his seat.

Rex came stampeding in, late as usual. All the desks shook as he went to his seat.

He glanced at the board.

MRS. D.'S BE'S were written there.

BE KIND, they said.

BE CURIOUS.

BE AWARE.

Rex pouted. "What happened to the ghost?" he asked.

"I guess the ghost has moved on," said Mrs. D. "Or maybe it's in 311 with Mr. Pterodactyl."

Rex slouched into his seat.

"What are we gonna do for fun?"

"You can always go to 311," said Hank eagerly.

*Swish-thump.*

"I'm sure we'll find something fu[...] Mrs. D. said. "After all, the year has just begun."

*** *** ***

Be sure to read the next Dino School book,
*Halloween Double Dare.*